Speak Koine Greek:

A Conversational Phrasebook

Speak Koine Greek:

A Conversational Phrasebook

T. Michael W. Halcomb
Fredrick J. Long

GlossaHouse ᏟᏂ
Wilmore, KY
www.GlossaHouse.com

GlossaHouse, LLC
110 Callis Circle
Wilmore, KY 40390

Halcomb, T. Michael W.
  Speak Koine Greek : a conversational phrasebook / T. Michael W. Halcomb, Fredrick J. Long. – Wilmore, KY : GlossaHouse, ©2014.

       32 pages ; 20 cm. – (Accessible Greek resources and online studies series. Reference)

       Includes bibliographical references.
       ISBN 9780615976273 (paperback)

       1. Greek language, Biblical – Conversation and phrase books – English. 2. Greek language, Biblical – Pronunciation.   I. Title. II. Series. III. Long, Fredrick J., 1966-

PA267.H34 2014

The fonts used to create this work are available from www.linguistsoftware.com/lgku.htm.

Cover Design by T. Michael W. Halcomb
Book Design by T. Michael W. Halcomb

To the students of the Conversational Koine Institute:
εὐχαριστοῦμεν τῷ θεῷ περὶ πάντων ὑμῶν.

AGROS

Accessible Greek Resources and Online Studies

AGROS

The Greek word ἀγρός is a field where seeds are planted and growth occurs. It can also denote a small village or community that forms around such a field. The type of community envisioned here is one that attends to Holy Scripture, particularly one that encourages the use of biblical Greek. Accessible Greek Resources and Online Studies (AGROS) is a tiered curriculum suite featuring innovative readers, grammars, specialized studies, and other exegetical resources to encourage and foster the exegetical use of biblical Greek. The goal of AGROS is to facilitate the creation and publication of innovative and inexpensive print and digital resources for the exposition of Scripture within the context of the global church. The AGROS curriculum includes five tiers, and each tier is indicated on the book's cover: Tier 1 (Beginning I), Tier 2 (Beginning II), Tier 3 (Intermediate I), Tier 4 (Intermediate II), and Tier 5 (Advanced). There are also two resource tracks: Conversational and Translational. Both involve intensive study of morphology, grammar, syntax, and discourse features. The conversational track specifically values the spoken word, and the enhanced learning associated with speaking a language in actual conversation. The translational track values the written word, and encourages analytical study to aide in understanding and translating biblical Greek and other Greek literature. The two resource tracks complement one another and can be pursued independently or together.

Table of Contents

Introduction   1-8

I. Beginning the Conversation   10-13
    A. Greetings   10
    B. Exclamations and Announcements   10-11
    C. Weather Conditions   11-12
    D. Initial Questions and Requests   12-13

II. Continuing the Conversation   13-27
    A. Time and Space Designators   13-14
    B. Transitions   14-15
    C. Making Statements   15
    D. Linking Thoughts Together   15-16
    E. Asking Questions to Clarify   16-21
    F. Answering Questions   21
    G. Commands and Requests   21-23
    H. Exclamations and Responses   3-25
    I. Various "I" Statements   25-27

III. Ending the Conversation   27-29

    A. Goodbyes   27-28

    B. Ancitipcating Future Arrangements   28

    C. Expressing Good Wishes/Blessings   28

    D. Greetings to Others   29

    E. Thanksgiving   29

Vocatives (Direct Address)   29-30

Asking Rhetorical Questions   30-31

Introduction

This *Conversational Phrasebook* is aimed at a particular audience, namely, those desiring to speak in Koine Greek idiom. Although this community remains small at the moment, it is quickly growing. Our hope is that in our lifetimes, this community will become a well-known and respected movement. We hope this book can benefit this group in particular and other students of Koine Greek in general. Our *Conversational Phrasebook* contains more than 225 conversational turns of phrase; yet it is different than the works of C. F. D. Moule and of Stanley Porter on New Testament idioms,[1] as well as the book on vocabulary and idiom by W. J. Bullick and J. A. Harrison that provides vocabulary based on the works of Euripides and Sophocles.[2] Our book is not a study on the origins of ancient idioms, how they form, or even how they work. Instead, this book is a compilation of phrases, expressions, and idioms to help learners of Koine Greek make progress in their fluency, and to have fun while doing it. As a supplement, companion audio files for this book are available for purchase at GlossaHouse.com.

In the introduction to *800 Words and Images: A New Testament Greek Vocabulary Builder* Halcomb stated,

An essential aspect of successfully navigating any foreign language is vocabulary acquisition. Acquiring the ability to comprehend, recall, and

---

1 C. F. D. Moule, *An Idiom Book of New Testament Greek* (2nd ed.; Cambridge University Press, 1959) and Stanley E. Porter, *Idioms of the Greek New Testament* (2nd ed.; Sheffield: Sheffield Academic Press, 1994).

2 W. J. Bullick and J. A. Harrison, *Greek Vocabulary and Idiom for Higher Forms* (London; New York: Macmillan; St Martin's Press, 1962; repr. London: Bristol Classical, 2004).

use vocabulary takes time and practice, whether in a communicative event involving two or more people or in a self-oriented activity such as reading.[3]

He showed that modern linguistic research supports this approach to the language learning process. In the same way, we would extend this perspective on language acquisition to learning idioms, phrases, and figures of speech. This, too, is rooted in modern language studies.

There is no need to provide a comprehensive overview of research supporting this claim here; however, a few words and references will prove beneficial. For example, even two decades ago in her research study and report to improve literacy for second language learners, *What Does That Mean? An Introduction to American Idioms*, Ellen McDevitt contended that idioms were not only a significant part of learning a language, but also an indicator of a student's level of fluency.[4] To anyone who has ever attempted to learn a second language, this much is likely obvious. Subsequent research continues to affirm the importance of learning idioms. For example, Eve Zyzik has noted, "The idea that formulaic sequences are an intrinsic part of linguistic competence has become widely accepted in the field of second language acquisition."[5] Such conclusions are to be expected, because numerous studies have shown that nearly 25% of everyday language use is idiomatic.[6]

---

3 T. Michael W. Halcomb, *800 Words and Images: A New Testament Greek Vocabulary Builder* (Wilmore, Ky.: GlossaHouse, 2013), 1.

4 Ellen McDevitt, *What Does That Mean? An Introduction to American Idioms* (Washington, D.C.: The Department of Education, 1993).

5 Eve Zyzik, "Second Language Idiom Learning: The Effects of Lexical Knowledge and Pedagogical Sequencing," *Language Teaching Research* 15 (2011): 413-33 at 414.

6 For sources see Christina Reuterskiold and Diana Van Lancker Sidtis, "Retention of Idioms Following One-Time Exposure," *Child Language Teaching and Therapy* 29 (2012): 219–31 at 220.

Although in common practice we use the words "idiom" or "idiomatic" with some sense of understanding, theoretical researchers still seek clarification. Zyzik admits that idioms are a "fuzzy category" that includes "semi-fixed multiword expressions" which may have "non-compositional features" (the meaning of an idiomatic phrase is not the sum of its component words) and/or "figurative meanings" (the meaning of an idiomatic phrase is possible by extending the meanings of individual words figuratively).[7] For this reason, idioms are easier for adults to learn than children, since they require more processing effort. Research suggests that figurative language becomes understandable around age six and from there it continues to develop.[8] For an adult already fluent in a language, however, the amount of time it takes to process idioms in a second language typically decreases. Perhaps part of the reason for this is that adults are easily more capable of segmenting figurative speech into mental groupings. Thomas C. Cooper's dictum is on target, "Dividing idioms into thematic categories will make them easier to learn, for the student can study them as groups composed of elements that have common features rather than as lists of unrelated expressions to be memorized."[9]

Our *Conversational Phrasebook* has been strategically arranged into categories to help students find common sayings, expressions, phrases, idioms, and figures of speech in ancient Greek, especially Koine Greek. For ease of use, our organization corresponds to the contour of an actual conversation: Beginning the Conversation, Continuing the Conversation, and Ending

---

7 Zyzik, "Second Language Idiom Learning," 415.

8 See *Vigo International Journal of Applied Linguistics* 8 (2011): 207-34).

9 Thomas C. Cooper, "Teaching Idioms," *Foreign Language Annals,* 31 (1998): 255-66 at 263.

the Conversation. Within each phase of the conversation, one finds several subcategories that correspond to topics, components, expressions, or strategies of conversation. The format of each entry begins with an English gloss translation that is followed by a phrase similar or comparable in Koine (with a few taken from classical Greek) and ends with a source citation. The great majority of the phrases or terms are attested in ancient literature. However, some are reconstructed; we think they may have been used but we have not found ancient attestation to their use. Consequently, we have created idiomatic equivalents to common English statements. Excepting this handful of phrases, for each entry we have cited ancient sources as the basis for the phrase.

We need also to qualify that not every idiom, phrase, or term included is found in the context of ancient conversation. If we had confined our research to such a small corpus, the results would have been rather meager and limited in scope. We have therefore found phrases from a variety of ancient genres, including narrative, history, poetry and letters. Regarding this latter genre, ancient letters were often thought of as representations of a person's actual presence (cf. 1 Cor 5.3, 9, 11); they functioned as surrogates for actual speech "in person." For example, when the first-century author Demetrius wrote his treatise *On Style*, he maintained that personal letters should imitate a conversational style (226). Therefore, terms like ἔρρωσθε, commonly occurring in letters, works well in reconstructing the way one might say "goodbye" in actual conversation. At the same time, we realize that there are terms, phrases, and idioms within ancient conversational pieces that have not been included here. If we are afforded the opportunity to create future editions of this *Conversational Phrasebook*, we will include more of these.

In addition, it should be noted that a few of the entries either predate or postdate the Koine era. This isn't unwarranted, however, since many ancient works were collected in libraries and continued to reflect and influence conversational practices. Recent studies have urged us to keep in mind the profoundly oral environment of the ancient Mediterranean world, which deeply impacted written texts.[10] So, as long as these entries do not violate Koine syntax, we find no problem including them here. This, in fact, would be our response to those who might ask, "Why not just go ahead and use Modern Greek?" In order to preserve and play by the rules of Koine syntax, we cannot "just go ahead" and do that. We should say, additionally, that a few of the Greek phrases have been slightly modified for our purposes here; yet these instances are so few and minor that we have not marked such entries in any way. In the end and to the best of our knowledge, all of the entries we have created would have been understandable, if not even at home, in the Koine era. Indeed, the bulk of our entries come from the Septuagint or New Testament. Outside of these primary sources, we have included phrases from the following: *Acts of Carpus*, Aesop, Antiphon, the Apocrypha, Aristophanes, Athenaeus, Cassius Dio, Demosthenes, Dionysius Halicarnassensis, Diogenes Laertius, Epictetus, Galen, Hermogenes, *Life of Aesop*, Lucian, Philo, Plato, Plutarch, Polyaenus, Sappho, and Xenophon.[11]

It may be helpful to consider our own experience

---

10   John H. Walton and D. Brent Sandy, *The Lost World of Scripture: Ancient Literary Culture and Biblical Authority* (Downers Grove, Ill.: IVP Academic, 2013).

11   We have used one inscriptional phrase catalogued by Étienne Bernand, *Inscriptions métriques de l'Égypte gréco-romaine. Recherches sur la poésie épigrammatique des Grecs en Égypte* (Annales littéraires de l'Université de Besançon 98; Paris, 1969).

of idioms. Each of us has our own conceptions of space and time; these impact our conception and use of idioms. Idiom is conventional usage that becomes standard practice and garners a semi-automatic or default deployment in specific social situations. Although it is true that we will never inhabit ancient Greece as the ancient Greeks did, still, as second language learners, we hope to gain an ever-increasing inner intuitive grasp of the Greek language. This is our goal. Social situations change, and so do languages; yet languages are adaptive to new social environments, while retaining core expressions that are transcultural or trans-temporal, e.g., greetings. This complexity of language use—its sustaining power of expression as well as its adaptation to new social environments—is reflective of our *Conversational Phrasebook*.

Of course, speaking in Greek requires that one is able to think in Greek. We will never fully recover the mindset and language capacities of the Koine Greek era; but we can do our best to recover certain dimensions of Koine Greek in terms of its conversational idiom. Our *Conversational Phrasebook* is an initial investigation that strives towards this end. In a nutshell, what we are doing is collecting idioms in an effort to assist those who desire to think and speak in Koine idiom, so that they can learn and use the language more creatively, effectively, and constructively. Indeed, one of the strengths of our approach here, which differentiates it from a traditional methodology focused on grammar and translation of written materials, is that our approach shows that the spoken living language is driving the grammatical constructions rather than the other way around. We are not saying that there is no value in traditional methodology; indeed, the grammar-translation method can help us more readily identify these discrete constructions and equip us to talk more clearly and astutely about them. But we would maintain that a conversational idiom-learning approach assists students to gain an insider's perspective on the pragmatic use of the Koine language by attending to the oral impact of utterance contained in the constructions themselves.[12]

In fact, the conception of this *Conversational Phrasebook* originated in the recurring interest of Halcomb's students at the Conversational Koine Institute (visit CKI at ConversationalKoine.com) to have a comparable way of saying something in Greek that might be commonly said in English or another primary language. Although we began researching ancient Greek expressions, we also considered common conversational topics and expressions in English, Spanish, and Modern Greek among others; from these latter, then, we returned to research again for equivalent ancient Greek expressions. However, we have attempted to avoid anachronism and to be fair in our glosses and translations/paraphrases.

Our inclusion of this or that conversational expression was not predicated on how many times it is attested in ancient Greek. For example, the expression πληρώσεις με εὐφροσύνης μετὰ τοῦ προσώπου σου is taken from Ps 16.11 and used in Acts 2.28. This statement is not attested much at all in ancient literature. Yet, it is a statement somewhat comparable to the English expression "It is great to see your face!" that is used when we are *really happy* to see someone. In this *Conversational Phrasebook*, we sometimes adjust idioms to match more closely our American English idiom; for example, we

---

12   Much more research is needed to relate grammar, pragmatics, and orality. GlossaHouse will continue to pursue and produce publications that reflect and encourage such research.

might modify a verb tense as we did with the phrase above from Acts, in order to arrive at ἐπλήρωσάς με εὐφροσύνης μετὰ τοῦ προσώπου σου. We deemed such license justifiable, since we know that the earliest Christians often used and adjusted idiom just as we do today. In fact, if you've ever said "Peace of Christ!" to your neighbor during a Sunday morning worship gathering, you have too.

Finally, we would like to thank GlossaHouse and the AGROS board for reviewing and accepting this work. As always, we would also like to acknowledge our families and their support during this project. We also would both like to thank our students, especially those who have encouraged us and taught us over the years. Our hope is that our near pocket-sized *Conversational Phrasebook* might be a blessing to all who read and use it, to help them think and speak in Koine Greek.

T. Michael W. Halcomb
&
Fredrick J. Long
Epiphany 2014

I. Beginning the Conversation

A. Greetings

Grace to you and peace - χάρις σοι καὶ εἰρήνη (2sg), χάρις ὑμῖν καὶ εἰρήνη (2pl) | 1 Thessalonians 1.1

Hello (esp. in the morning) - χαῖρε (2sg), χαίρετε (2pl) | Matthew 26.49

It is good to hear from you - καλόν μοι ἀκουεῖν τὴν φωνήν σου | cf. Song of Solomon 2.14

It is nice to meet you - πληροῖς με εὐφροσύνης μετὰ τοῦ προσώπου σου | Acts 2.28

B. Exclamations and Announcements ^(See Pg. 30 Note 1)

Alas! - οἴμμοι | Joel 1:15

Good day! - ὦ καλῆς ἡμέρας | cf. Plutarch, *Cleomenes* 30.2; Mod. Gr. καλημέρα

Eureka! (lit: I have found it!) - εὕρηκα | 2 John 1:4

Fire! - ἰδοὺ...πῦρ | 2 Kings 1.14 (LXX 4 Kings 1:14)

Hooray Hooray - ἰοῦ ἰοῦ | Aristophanes, *Peace* 345

It is meal time - ἀρίστου ὥρα ἐστίν | Susanna 1.13 (LXX Theodotian)

Many blessings to you - πόλλ' ἀγαθὰ γένοιτό σοι |
Aristophanes, *Women in Politics* 1067

Oh no! - ἰοὺ ἰού | Plutarch, *Theseus* 22.45

Terrible circumstances! - φαῦλα πράγματα or κακὰ
πράγματα | cf. Dionysius Halicarnassensis, *On Literary
Composition* 3.72 and LXX Sirach 11:33

Ugh! - αἰβοῖ | Aristophanes, *Clouds* 877

Well done! (or: Congratulations!) - εὖγε | Luke 19.17

C. Weather Conditions

A big hailstorm is coming - χάλαζα μεγάλη (ἔρχεται) |
cf. Revelation 11:19

It is a snowy day - ἡμέρα τῆς χιόνος (ἐστιν) | cf. 2
Samuel 23.20

It is bad weather today - σήμερον χειμών (ἐστιν) |
Matthew 16.3

It is cold - ψῦχός ἐστιν | cf. John 18.18

It is going to rain (lit: rain is coming) - ὄμβρος ἔρχεται
| Luke 12.54

It is hot - καύσων ἔστιν | cf. Luke 12.55

It is raining - γίνεται ὄμβρος | cf. Luke 12.54

11

It is windy (lit: there is wind) - γίνεται ἄνεμος | cf. Mark 4.37

There is lightning and thunder - γίνονται ἀστραπαὶ καὶ βρονταί | Revelation 11.19

The sky is clear - ὁ οὐρανὸς τῇ καθαριότητι (ἐστιν) | cf. Exodus 24.10

The weather is nice - εὐδία (ἐστιν) | Matthew 16.2

D. Initial Questions and Requests

Are you hungry? - πεινῇς; | Reconstructed (Unattested)

Are you thirsty? - διψᾷς; | Reconstructed (Unattested)

Are you married? - γαμεῖς; | Lucian, *Dialogues of the Courtesans* 2.3.1

How are you? - πῶς ἔχεις; (2sg), πῶς ἔχετε; (2pl) | Athenaeus, *Deipnosophistae* 8.24.43

Do you know/speak Greek? - Ἑλληνιστὶ γινώσκεις; | Acts 21.37

May I (say something to you)? - εἰ ἔξεστίν μοι (εἰπεῖν τι πρὸς σέ); | Acts 21.37

May I ask you something? - πυνθάνομαι τι παρά σου; | cf. Acts 10.29

Show us the way to the city - δεῖξον ἡμῖν τὴν εἴσοδον τῆς πόλεως | Judges 1.24

Tell me your name - ἀνάγγειλόν μοι τὸ ὄνομά σου | Genesis 32.29 (LXX Genesis 32.30)

What are you reading? - τί ἀναγινώσκεις; | cf. acts 8:30

What are you studying? - τί σπουδάζεις; | Cassius Dio, *Roman History* 14.4

What can I do for you? (alt: Can I help you?) - τί ποιήσω σοι; | 2 Kings 4.2 (LXX 4 Kings 4.2)

What do you know? - τί γινώσκεις; | cf. Galen, *On the Method of Healing*, 14.10.100.2

What is your job? - τίς σου ἡ ἐργασία ἐστίν; | Jonah 1.8

What is your name? - τί ὄνομα σοι; | Mark 5.9

Where's the bathroom? - ποῦ ὁ ἀφεδρών (ἐστιν); | Reconstructed (Unattested)

II. Continuing the Conversation

A. Time and Space Designators

A little while - ὡς μικρόν or δι᾽ ὀλίγου | 2 Chronicles 12.7; Josephus *Jewish Antiquities* 5.319

In the middle - ἐν μέσῳ | Genesis 3.3

It is getting late - τῆς ὥρας γίνεται ὀψέ | cf. Demosthenes, *Oratio in Midiam* 21.84

Near the _ (or: Next to the _) - ἐγγὺς τοῦ ___ (always with the genitive) | John 6.19

Now - νῦν (or: for more emphasis: ὁ νῦν καιρός) | Romans 3.26

Tomorrow... - εἰς (ἐπὶ) τὴν αὔριον | Luke 10.35; Acts 4.3

To the east - κατὰ ἀνατολάς | Deuteronomy 3.27

To the left - εἰς ἀριστερόν | Genesis 13.9

To the north - κατὰ βορρᾶν | Deuteronomy 3.27

To the right - εἰς δεξιόν | Genesis 13.9

To the south - κατὰ λίβα | Deuteronomy 3.27

To the west - κατὰ δυσμάς | Numbers 33.49

B. Transitions

After this... (sg), these things (pl.)... - μετὰ τοῦτο... (sg), μετὰ ταῦτα... (pl) | Genesis 10.18

Because of this... - διὰ τοῦτο... | Genesis 11.9

Now concerning... - περὶ δέ... | 1 Corinthians 7:1

Rarely (or: Seldom) - σπανίως | Xenophon, *Ageselius* 9.1

Until now.../up to this point... - ἄχρι τοῦ νῦν... | Philippians 1.5

What's remaining... - τὸ λοιπὸν... | 2 Thessalonians 3:1

C. Making Statements

It is not possible... - οὐ δύναται... | Job 6.7

It seems to me - μοι δοκεῖ (or: δοκεῖ μοι) | Acts 25.27

I think (that)... - δοκῶ (ὅτι)... | Epictetus, *Discourses* 1.1.8

I/we know (that)... - οἶδα/οἴδαμεν (ὅτι)... | Matthew 22:16

Surely... (or: Truly...) - ἀληθῶς ... | Matthew 26.73

What you are doing is wrong (or: You are not doing it the right way) - οὐκ ὀρθῶς σὺ ποιεῖς | cf. Exodus 18.17

D. Linking Thoughts Together

And once again... - πάλιν τε αὖ... | Diogenes Laertius, *Lives of Philosophers* 9.9

Etcetera (etc.) - καὶ τὰ λοιπά (abbrev: κτλ.) | Athenaeus, *Deipnosophistae* 15.60.108

So to speak - ὡς ἔπος εἰπεῖν | Plato, *Gorgias* 450d

Unless... - εἰ μὴ... (or: ἐὰν μὴ...) | Genesis 31.42 (or: Genesis 43.3)

E. Asking Questions to Clarify (See Pg. 31 Note 2)

And you? - καὶ σύ; | Diogenes Laertius, *Lives of Philosophers* 2.68.3

Are you not talking to me? - ἐμοὶ οὐ λαλεῖς; | John 19.10

Are you (traveling) alone? - σὺ μόνος; | cf. 1 Samuel 21.2 (21.1 in some versions)

At what time exactly? - πηνίκ᾽ ἐστὶν ἄρα τῆς ἡμέρας; | Aristophanes, *Birds* 1498

Can you hear? (or: Are you listening?) _ ἀκούεις; (2sg), ἀκούετε; (2pl) | Matthew 21.16

Come again? - πάλιν; | cf. John 9.27

Do you have a brother or sister? - ἔχει ἀδελφὸν ἢ ἀδελφήν; | cf. Genesis 44.19

Do you have children? - τέκνα ἔχεις; | Acts of Carpus, *Papylus and Agathonice* 28.1

Do you know about__? - τί γινώσκεις περὶ __; | Plutarch, *Brutus* 40.6.4

Do you know him/it? - γινώσκεις αὐτόν/αὐτό; | cf.
Plutarch, *Sayings of Kings and Commanders* 186a.11

Do you understand? - γινώσκεις; (sg.), γινώσκετε; (pl.)
| John 13.12

Do you want to... (+ infinitive)? - θέλεις...; | John 5:6

For what reason? (or: Why?) - ἵνα τί; | Genesis 4.6

How? - πῶς; | Genesis 44.34

How can I be sure about this? - κατὰ τί γνώσομαι
τοῦτο; | Luke 1.18

How did you get here? - πῶς ἦλθες; | Athenaeus,
Deipnosophistae 3.81

How do I get there? - ποίᾳ ὁδῷ πορεύσομαι; | cf. 1
Kings 13.12

How (lit: from where) do you know me? - πόθεν με
γινώσκεις; | John 1.48

How do you say...? - πῶς λέγεις...; | Judges 16.15

How does it look to you all? - πῶς ὑμεῖς βλέπετε αὐτόν;
| cf. Haggai 2.3

How far? - πόσος; | Xenophon, *Cyropaedia* 6.3.10.2

How long...? - ἕως πότε...; | 1 Samuel 1.14

How many? - πόσοι; | Matthew 15.34
17

How many times? - ποσάκις; | 1 Kings 22.16

How much do I owe? - πόσον ὀφείλω; | cf. Luke 16.5

How old are you? - πόσα ἔτη ἡμερῶν τῆς ζωῆς σου; | Genesis 47.8

May I say something to you? - εἰ ἔξεστίν μοι εἰπεῖν τι πρὸς σέ; | Acts 21.37

May I ask you something? - πυνθάνομαι τὶ παρά σου; | cf. Acts 10.29

Me too - κἀμέ | Exodus 12.32

Really? - ἄληθες; | Aristophanes, *Frogs* 840

So you're saying...? - φής...; | Lucian, *Dialogue of the Gods* 1:1

What? - τί; | Hebrews 11.32

What can/should I say? (lit: What will I say?) - τί ἐρῶ; | cf. Joshua 7.8

What did you say? - τί εἶπας; | cf. Genesis 26:9

What do you have? - τί ἔχεις; | 1 Corinthians 4.7

What do you see? - τί σὺ ὁρᾷς; | Jeremiah 1.13

What do you think? - τί δοκεῖς; | Epictetus, *Discourses* 1.26.6.1

What do you want? - τί θέλεις; | Matthew 20.21

What does __ mean? - τί δύναται __ ; | Athenaeus, *Deipnosophistae* 9.29.44

What does this mean? - τί θέλει τοῦτο εἶναι; | Acts 2.12

What else...? - τί ἄλλο....; | Malachi 2.15

What have you done? - τί τοῦτο ἐποίησας; | Genesis 3.13

What's the matter/wrong with you? - τί πάσχεις; | Aristophanes, *Clouds* 877

What's the temperature? - τί ἡ κρᾶσις τοῦ ἀέρος (ἐστιν); | cf. Plutarch, *The Obsolescence of Oracles* 435b8

What's up? (lit: What are you doing?) - τί ποιεῖς; | Judges 18.3

What is it? - τί ἐστιν; | Genesis 21.17

What is this? - τί ἐστιν τοῦτο; | Mark 1.27

What is your interpretation (of what you're reading)? - πῶς ἀναγινώσκεις; | Luke 10.26

What kind (or: What sort of)...? - ποταπός...; | Matthew 8.27

What time is it? - πηνίκα μάλιστα; | Lucian, *Solecisms* 5

When...? - πότε...; | Genesis 30.30

Where...? - ποῦ...; | Isaiah 19.12

Where are you coming from? - πόθεν ἔρχη; | Jonah 1.8

Where are you from? - πόθεν εἶ σύ; | 2 Samuel 1.13

Where are we going? - ποῦ ἡμεῖς ἀναβαίνομεν; | Deuteronomy 1.28

Where are you going? - ποῦ ὑπάγεις; | John 16.15

Where can I go to get away from you? - ἀπὸ τοῦ προσώπου σου ποῦ φύγω; | Psalm 138.7 LXX

Whether ... or...? (i.e. which one (of two)?) - πότερον ... ἤ; | Job 7.12

Who? - τίς; | 1 John 2.22

Whose...? - τίνος...; | Mark 12.16

Who are you? - σὺ τίς εἶ; | James 4.12

Who is that person? - τίς ἐστιν ὁ ἄνθρωπος ἐκεῖνος; | Genesis 24.65

Who told you __? - τίς σοι εἶπεν ὅτι __; | Cassius Dio, *Roman History* 60.33.8

Why? - (διὰ) τί; | 2 Corinthians 11.11

Why are you sad? - τί γὰρ λυποῦμαι; | *Life of Aesop* (W) 25.3 (3rd Recension)

Why did you say...? -- τί εἶπας; | cf. Genesis 26:9

Why not? - πῶς γὰρ οὔ; | Athenaeus, *Deipnosophistae* 3.74.15

F. Answering Questions
(see also below under "I" Statements)

He/she is not here - οὐκ ἔστιν ὧδε | Matthew 28.6

Most likely... - εἰκότως γε | Philo, *On Dreams* 1.247

No! - οὐχί | Luke 16.30

No thank you (lit: I'm excellent, I commend you) - κάλλιστ᾽, ἐπαινῶ | Aristophanes, *Frogs* 508

No way! - μὴ γένοιτο | 1 Corinthians 6.15

G. Commands and Requests

Answer me! - δός μοι ἀπόκρισιν | Job 33.5

Be quiet! - σιώπησον (2sg), σιωπήσατε (2pl) | Epictetus, *Discourses* 1.2.20.1

Come back! - ἐπίστρεψον (2sg), ἐπιστρέψατε (2pl) | 2 Samuel 14.21

Come have a meal (lit: lunch) - δεῦτε ἀριστήσατε | John 21.12

Come here! - ἐλθὲ ἐνθάδε | John 4.16

Come, share a meal with me - εἴσελθε μετ᾽ ἐμοῦ...καὶ ἀρίστησον | 1 Kings 13.7

Continue! (or: Keep doing...!) - διατέλει (sg.), διατελεῖτε (pl.) | Acts 27:33

Don't be afraid! - μὴ φοβοῦ | Genesis 15.1

Forgive me (please) - συγγνώμην ἔχε | Sirach 3.13

Forgive me for this wrong - χαρίσασθέ μοι τὴν ἀδικίαν ταύτην | 2 Corinthians 12.13

Get some rest! - ἀνάπαυσον (2sg), ἀναπαύσασθε (2pl) | Mark 6.31

Get up! - ἀνάστηθι (2sg), ἀνάστητε (2pl) | 2 Samuel 13.15

Get out! - ἀπόστα | Gen 19.9

Give me a drink - δός μοι πεῖν | John 4.10

Go! - πορεύου (2sg), πορεύεσθε (2pl) | Exodus 2.8

Go away! - ἀπόστηθι (2sg), ἀπόστητε (2pl) | Lamentations 4.15

Go on! (or: Come on!) - ἄγε | James 5:1

Listen (up)! - ἄκουσον (2sg), ἀκούσατε (2pl) | Genesis 23.6

Listen to me now! - νῦν…ἄκουσόν μου | Exodus 18.19
Look! - ἰδού | Genesis 1.29

Please excuse me - ἔχε με παρῃτημένον | Luke 14.19

Praise God! - εὐλογητὸς ὁ θεός | Psalm 65.20 (66.20 in some versions)

Praise the Lord! - εὐλογητὸς κύριος | Luke 1.68

Save me! - σῶσόν με | Psalm 11.1 (12.1 in some versions)

Sit down! - κάθισον (2sg), καθίσατε (2pl) | Jeremiah 48.14

Stop! (another person; a thing) - παῦσον (2sg), παύσατε (2pl) | Psalm 34.14

Stop! (yourself; doing something) - παῦσαι (2sg), παύσασθε (2pl) | Exodus 32.12

So tell me… - εἰπέ (or: λέγε) μοι | John 20.15 (or: Acts 22.27)

H. Exclamations and Responses

Amen - ἀμήν | Matthew 5.18

Correct (or: straight) - ὀρθῶς | cf. Genesis 4:7

Excellent! - θαυμαστόν | Revelation 15.1

Great idea! - μέγεθος ἰδεῶν (or: μάλιστα τῆς ἰδέας) |
Hermogenes, *On Style* 169-70, 172

Help us! - βοήθησον ἡμῖν | Joshua 10.6

Incorrect (or: bad) - κακῶς | cf. John 18:23

Indeed! - ἀμέλει | Polyaenus, *War Strategies* 2.22.3

Kudos! (lit: Glory to you!) - κῦδος | Isaiah 14.25

Maybe - τάχα | Philemon 1.15

Nevermind - ἀμέλει | Aristophanes, *Clouds* 877

So far so good (or: Great!) - εἶέν | Antiphon, *Tetrology*
4.2.3

Surely... (or: Truly...) - ἀληθῶς... | Matthew 26.73

Terrible circumstances! - φαῦλα πράγματα | Dionysius
Halicarnassensis, *On Literary Composition* 3.72

These things do not please me - ταῦτά μοι οὐκ ἀρέσκει
| Esther 5.13

Very nice! - ὡς ἡδύ | Plutarch, *Life of Pyrrhus* 27.9

Yes - ναί | Genesis 17.19

Wait! - ὑπόμεινον (2sg), ὑπομείνατε (2pl) | Psalm 26.14
(27.14 in some translations)

Wait a minute - μεῖνόν με μικρὸν ἔτι | Job 36.2

I. Various "I" Statements

I am alone - ἐγὼ μόνος εἰμί | Tobit 6:15

I am (doing) good/well - καλῶς ἔχω (or: εὖ ἔχω) | Reconstructed (Unattested)

I am happy (now) - νῦν χαίρω | 2 Corinthians 7.9

I am here - ἰδοὺ ἐγώ | Genesis 27.1

I am here with __ (lit: This is __.) - οὗτός ἐστιν __. (masc., 2sg), αὕτη ἐστιν __. (fem., 2sg) | Matthew 3.17

I am hungry - πεινῶ | Reconstructed (Unattested)

I am leaving/going tomorrow - αὔριον πορεύομαι | James 4.13

I am not alone - οὐκ εἰμὶ μόνος | John 16.32

I am not going to wait for you - οὐχ οὕτως μενῶ ἐνώπιόν σου | 2 Samuel 18.14

I am not (doing) good/well - κακῶς ἔχω (or: οὐ καλῶς ἔχω) | Menander, *Dyscolus* Line 55

I am (not) sick - (οὐκ) ἀσθενῶ | 2 Corinthians 11.29

I am (not) sorry - (οὐ) μεταμέλομαι | 2 Corinthians 7.8

I am sad - λυποῦμαι | Aesop, *Fables* 81.21

I am sleepy - νυστάζω | Proverbs 24.33

I am thirsty - διψῶ | John 19.28

I am worn out/tired - κοπιῶ | Isaiah 33.24

I can (+ infinitive)... – δύναμαι... | Matthew 9:28

I cannot (+ infinitive)... - οὐ δύναμαι... | John 5:30

I come from ___. - ἐγὼ ἐκ τῶν ___ εἰμί. | John 8.23

I do not know - οὐκ οἶδα | Matthew 26.70

I do not like... - οὐ φιλῶ... | Athenaeus, *Deipnosophistae* 9.29.44

I do not understand/know - οὐ γινώκσω | Romans 7.15

I do not understand what you are saying - οὐκ ἐπίσταμαι σὺ τί λέγεις | Mark 14.68

I don't want... - οὐ θέλω... | 1 Corinthians 10.20

I found... - εὗρον... | Genesis 26.19

I have a question for you - ἐρωτήσω σε | Job 42.4

I have been/was here before - ἤμην ἐν τῷ τόπῳ | John 19.14

I have forgiven you - κεχάρισμαί σοι | 2 Corinthians 2.10

I hope to (+ infinitive) - ἐλπίζω...ἰδεῖν | 3 John 1:14

I live in... - κατοικῶ ἐν... | 2 Samuel 7.2

I live with... - κατοικῶ μετά... | 1 Kings 17.20

I love you - φιλῶ σε | John 21.17

I need... (lit: I have need of...) - ἐγὼ ἔχω χρείαν... | cf. Matthew 3.14

I understand/know - γινώσκω | 1 Corinthians 13.12

I want to (+ infinitive)... - θέλω... | 1 Corinthians 7:32

I will say it again... - πάλιν ἐρῶ... | Philippians 4.4

I wish (that)... (+ infinitive) - θέλω... | John 21:22

I would like... (+ infinitive) - θέλω... | 1 Corinthians 7:32

Just as/like I like it - ὡς φιλῶ | Genesis 27.9

III. Ending the Conversation

A. GoodByes

Goodbye, bye - ἔρρωσο (2sg), ἔρρωσθε (2pl) | Acts 15.29

Good night (lit: Sweet sleep/dream) - γλυκὺς ὕπνος |
Ecclesiastes 5.12; (alt: καλὴ νύξ - unattested); Mod. Gr.
καληνύκτα

It was nice meeting you - ἐπλήρωσας με εὐφροσύνης
μετὰ τοῦ προσώπου σου | Acts 2.28

I hope to see you soon - | ἐλπίζω εὐθέως σε ἰδεῖν | 3 Jn
1:14

B. Anticipating Future Arrangements

Prepare a room for me - ἑτοίμαζέ μοι ξενίαν | Philemon
1.22

You are welcome to stay at my home (2pl) - εἰσελθόντες
εἰς τὸν οἶκόν μου μένετε | Acts 16.15

C. Expressing Good Wishes/Blessings

I hope you have a good trip - καὶ σοὶ εὐδίης τρίβον
ὄλβιον εὔχομαι εἶναι | *Extant Greek and Roman
Inscriptions* 5 (Bernand)

Get well! - ἰῶ (sg.), ἰᾶσθε (pl.) | Galen, *On Sects*, 1.91.6

Happy travels! - χαίροισ' ἔρχεο | Sappho, 23.7 (Diehl,
Papyrus Fragments)

May it go well with you - εὖ σοι γένηται | Genesis 40.14

D. Greetings to others

I/they send you all greetings - | ἀσπάζομαι ὑμᾶς (1 sg.) ἀσπάζονται ὑμᾶς (2 sg.) | 2 Corinthians 13.12

E. Thanksgiving

Thank you (lit: I thank you) - εὐχαριστῶ (σοι) | Luke 18.11

It's nothing to me (alt: You're welcome, no thanks) - οὐδὲν διαφέρει | Diogenes Laertius, *Lives of Philosophers* 1.36.1 (cf. "No thank you" at II.f. above.)

My pleasure (lit: This pleases me) - τοῦτό μοι ἀρέσκει | cf. Esther 5.13

[1] Vocatives (Direct Address)

When speaking, it is common to address people directly. In Greek, the persons addressed directly are placed into the vocative case (κλητικὴ πτῶσις), usually near the beginning of the sentence. If the name is undeclinable, then there is no change. However, if the person's or group's name is declinable, then you will need to convert the name into the vocative case. The chart below provides the vocative endings.

The vocative case endings in the plural for all genders of nouns are the same as the nominative endings. In the singular, however, the vocative form is different. Here are the basic rules.

Formation of the Vocative Case							
Feminine Sg.			Masculine Sg.			Neuter Sg.	
1 Decl.	2 Decl.	3 Decl.	1 Decl.	2 Decl.	3 Decl.	2 Decl.	3 Decl.
-α or -η	-ε	none pure stem	-α or -η	-ε	none pure stem	-ον	-ν or none

Note: For some 3rd declension nouns with the final syllable -η, the final vowel in the stem will change in the vocative form to -ε. Thus, πατήρ "father," μήτηρ "mother," θυγάτηρ "daughter," and ἀνήρ "husband" become in the vocative singular πάτερ, μῆτερ, θύγατερ, and ἄνερ (notice, too, the change of accent stress).

Sometimes you can add ὦ/῏Ω ("O") for added effect. Compare/contrast the following examples:

"And you Bethlehem, Land of Judah,..." - καὶ σὺ Βηθλέεμ, γῆ Ἰούδα,... | Matthew 2:6

"O Foolish Galatians,..." - ῏Ω ἀνόητοι Γαλάται,... | Galatians 3:1

"O Timothy, ..." - ῏Ω Τιμόθεε,... | 1 Timothy 6:20

[2] Asking Rhetorical Questions

It is possible to ask questions that expect a negative or positive answer. Such questions are rhetorical questions.

The negative words οὐ, οὐκ, or οὐχί are placed at the beginning of a question and expect a positive answer, with the later οὐχί being more emphatic. The negative words μή and μήτι are placed at the beginning of a question and expect a negative answer, with the later μήτι being more emphatic. For example:

Were not ten cleansed? (yes!) - οὐχὶ οἱ δέκα ἐκαθαρίσθησαν; | Luke 17.17

This guy isn't the Christ, is he? (no!) - μήτι οὗτός ἐστιν ὁ χριστός; | John 4.29

GlossaHouse
Wilmore, KY   G
                  H
www.GlossaHouse.com

Made in the USA
Middletown, DE
08 August 2021

45636633R00027